ESTATE PLANNING FOR GAY AND LESBIAN COUPLES

How to Get Your Affairs in Order
And Achieve Peace of Mind

JULIE A. CALLIGARO

ISBN: 1-890117323
ISBN-13: 978-1890117320

WHY READ THIS BOOK

Most of us avoid *estate planning*, which is another name for getting our affairs in order, until we face a life-changing event such as:

The birth or adoption of a child; the diagnosis of an illness that threatens disability or death; a family member or close friend dies unexpectedly. And sometimes it's just because we're about to take a trip.

But as a gay or lesbian couple, at least in most states, you're already facing a crisis because you don't have the benefit of laws that protect one partner at the disability and/or death of the other.

I congratulate you because you've decided to take action rather than wait for the crisis or emergency. This book will help you get your affairs in order, make things as easy as possible for you and your partner at incapacity and/or death and bring you peace of mind.

This book does NOT include fill-in-the-blank Wills, Trusts, Powers of Attorney or Guardianship forms. If you want a do-it-yourself estate plan this is not the book for you. In my 30 years as an estate planning and probate attorney, I've seen only regret and heartache from do-it-yourself legal forms.

I have, however, developed forms and checklists that will save you time and energy as you work through the estate planning process. The forms and checklists are free at www.wsbforms.com/single/. Download the forms and checklists and use them as you work through the action steps in each Chapter.

TABLE OF CONTENTS

THE ESTATE PLANNING STEPS

Step 1. Have Your Financial Information at Your Fingertips.

Step 2. Learn About the Estate Planning Tools:

- Wills
- Trusts
- Powers of Attorney
- Living Will
- Beneficiary Designation
- Joint Ownership

Step 3. Consider the Issues Unique to Your Situation. Do you have?

- Minor Children
- Adult Children
- No Children

Step 4. Choose an Estate Planning or Elder Law Attorney and Schedule an Appointment.

Step 5. Follow Through.

List of Forms and Checklists:

To download the forms and checklists click on:
www.wsbforms.com/single/

Forms Related to Finances

Excel Spreadsheet of Assets and Debts

Insurance Policies Inventory

Pension Plans Inventory

Forms Related to Minor Children

Parental Consent Form Minor Children

Medical Information Minor Children

At Disability and Death

Who to Contact in an Emergency

Location of Your Documents

Family Advisors

Funeral and Burial Information

Take to the Meeting with an Estate Planning Attorney

Questions to Ask the Attorney

Estate Planning Questionnaire

Excel Spreadsheet of Assets and Debts

Insurance Policies Inventory

Pension Plans Inventory

Checklist of Documents

Optional but Useful
Excel Spreadsheet of Income and Expenses

ONE

HOW TO HAVE YOUR FINANCIAL INFORMATION AT YOUR FINGERTIPS

This book is a practical guide to estate planning. But to formulate a complete and accurate estate plan, you need to begin with your financial information. Here's why.

It's impossible for you and your attorney to create an intelligent estate plan that transfers your assets at your death if you don't know precisely what assets you have. It's impossible for you and your attorney to be certain that your beneficiary designations are up-to-date if you don't know who the current beneficiaries are. And it's impossible to determine if your assets are titled correctly if you're not sure whose name or names are on the titles.

That's why to establish an accurate and complete estate plan, you need a list or inventory of your assets and debts which includes the name or names currently on the title of each asset. And you need a list or inventory of your life insurance policies and your retirement plans including the names of the primary and secondary beneficiaries.

Fortunately there are forms that will help you prepare these lists at www.wsbforms.com/single.

Download and complete the forms listed below. They are self-explanatory and worth the time it will take you to fill in the information.

- Excel Spreadsheet of Assets and Debts
- Insurance Policies Inventory
- Pension Plans Inventory

If you ignore everything else except this one Chapter, the book will have paid for itself.

TWO

WHO WILL MANAGE YOUR FINANCES AND MAKE MEDICAL DECISIONS FOR YOU?

You will discuss this issue in detail with your attorney. This Chapter will help you prepare for that discussion.

Who will manage your finances if you become incapacitated?

You can appoint your partner to manage your finances if you become incapacitated with a financial power of attorney or a living trust.

Financial Power of Attorney

A financial power of attorney is a legal document that appoints someone you TRUST as your "agent" should you become incapacitated. You may need this person to pay your bills, do your banking, file your tax returns, collect rents, etc. A power of attorney takes effect either at the time you sign the document <u>or</u> at the time you become incompetent. Be sure to discuss these options with your attorney.

Four Important Points About Financial Powers of Attorney:

1. You cannot sign a Power of Attorney if you are incompetent, so advance planning is essential.

2. A Power of Attorney gives your agent the power and authority over your finances, so you must choose a person you **trust.**

3. Name an alternate in case the first person you name is not available or able to act as your agent.

4. A Power of Attorney terminates at your death.

Living Trust (which is discussed in detail in the next Chapter)

A living trust is an alternative to a financial power of attorney because if you become disabled or incompetent, your successor trustee is authorized to take over the management of the trust assets during your disability or incompetence.

Who Will Make Medical Decisions for You if You Cannot Make Them for Yourself?

Medical Power of Attorney

A medical power of attorney is a legal document that appoints someone you TRUST to make medical decisions for you if you cannot make the decisions for yourself. You can appoint your partner, family member or friend. A medical power of attorney is also known as health care proxy and patient advocate designation.

Four Important Points About Medical Powers of Attorney:

1. You cannot sign a Power of Attorney if you are incompetent, so advance planning is essential.

2. A Power of Attorney gives your agent the power and authority to make your medical decisions, so you must choose a person you **trust.**

3. Name an alternate in case the first person you name is not available or able to act as your agent.

4. A Power of Attorney terminates at your death.

Living Will

A living will is a document that expresses your wishes concerning the use of artificial or life-support measures if there is no reasonable expectation you will recover.

I strongly recommend that you have a face to face discussion about end of life decisions with the people you appoint as your medical power of attorney. If your partner, family member or friend has to make a "turn off the machine" decision, it will be easier for them if you've told them how you feel and what you want and expect them to do.

Estate Plan

Financial and Medical Powers of Attorney are two of the documents included in an "Estate Plan." The other Estate Plan documents are discussed in the next Chapters.

Action Plan

- Your attorney will prepare the necessary documents that will appoint someone you trust either by a Power of Attorney or by a Living Trust to manage your finances if you become incapacitated or incompetent.
- Your attorney will prepare the necessary documents that will appoint someone you trust to make medical decisions for you if you cannot make the decisions for yourself.
- Have a face to face conversation with the people you've named as your medical power of attorney.

THREE

HOW TO TRANSFER ASSETS AT YOUR DEATH

YOU HAVE OPTIONS

You will discuss this issue in detail with your attorney. This Chapter will help you prepare for that discussion.

There are five ways to transfer assets at death:

1. Beneficiary Designation;

2. Joint Ownership;

3. Will;

4. No Will;

5. Living Trust.

Some combination of these documents, together with Financial and Medical Powers of Attorney, constitute an "Estate Plan."

1. Beneficiary Designation

Certain types of assets allow you to name a beneficiary who will receive the asset at your death. Assets that pass by beneficiary designation go directly to the beneficiary thereby avoiding Probate.

However, if your beneficiary dies before you and you have not named a secondary (also called contingent) beneficiary the asset must go through Probate.

Examples of assets that allow you to name a beneficiary are: life insurance policies, annuities, IRAs, and certain types of bank and brokerage accounts. Bank and brokerage accounts that allow you to name a beneficiary or beneficiaries are called "Transfer on Death" (TOD) or "Pay on Death" (POD).

2. Joint Ownership

If an asset is titled in your name and the name of another person as "joint tenants with rights of survivorship," the asset passes directly to your joint tenant(s) at your death thereby avoiding Probate. Examples are deeds, bank and brokerage accounts, savings bonds and stock certificates.

If, however, your joint tenant dies before you die, the asset will then be in your name alone. Unless you add a new joint tenant, the asset must go through Probate at your death.

There are risks and disadvantages holding an asset as a joint tenant.. They are:

1. To sell the asset you must have your joint tenant's cooperation and participation. For example, if you are selling your house and your partner is a joint tenant, he or she must also "sign off" before you will be able to complete the sale.

2. The asset is vulnerable to your joint tenant's lawsuits and creditors. For example, if your partner is a joint tenant on your bank account and she is sued, her creditors can collect from your bank account.

3. If you and your partner own property as joint tenants and your relationship terminates, you cannot remove your partner's name from the title unless he or she "signs off."

3. Will

If your assets pass to your designated beneficiary or beneficiaries by Will, THE ASSETS MUST GO THROUGH PROBATE. The preceding sentence may surprise you as most people believe that if they have a Will, they have avoided Probate. Not true. If assets pass by Will, they must go through Probate.

Why so? If, at your death, there are assets in your name alone, only a Probate Court can legally transfer those assets to the persons named in your Will.

The purpose of a Will is to tell the Probate Court who is to receive your assets at your death, who is to administer your estate (the personal representative or executor) and who is to be guardians of minor children.

4. No Will

If, at your death, there are assets in your name alone and you do not have a Will, your assets must pass through Probate and the laws of the state in which you live will dictate who will receive them.

5. Living Trust

A Living Trust is similar to a Will because it names who is to receive your assets at your death and who is to administer the Trust (the trustee).

You create a Living Trust by signing a legal document called a Trust Agreement. You are the trust maker, the trustee and the beneficiary. You can change or revoke your trust at any time.

As the trustee and beneficiary you manage and have full use of the trust assets during your lifetime. If you become incompetent and at your death, the person you have named as your successor trustee takes over.

A living trust is especially useful if your become disabled or incapacitated because your successor trustee is authorized to take over the management of the trust assets. If a successor trustee does take over because of your illness or incapacity, the trust assets are used *exclusively* for your support and care.

A Trust CAN Avoid Probate

At your death your successor trustee distributes the assets to the person or persons you've named as the beneficiaries of your trust. If your assets are in the name of your Trust, the assets will pass directly to the trust beneficiaries avoiding Probate. However, if your assets are not in the name of your Trust, the assets must first go through Probate to get to your trust beneficiaries.

Your attorney will transfer your assets to your trust by changing the title of the asset from your name into the name of your trust. If you have a trust but your assets have not been transferred into the trust, contact your attorney immediately.

The primary difference between a will and a trust is a trust can avoid probate. A will cannot avoid probate.

Other Reasons to Use a Living Trust

Trusts are used for reasons other than avoiding probate, for example: trusts are used to safeguard distributions to minor children and to safeguard governmental benefits that are or may be received by disabled children and/or adults.

Avoiding Probate

You will avoid Probate if:

1. Your assets pass by beneficiary designation and the beneficiary survives you.

2. You hold title as joint tenant with right of survivorship and the joint tenant survives you.

3. You have a living trust and your assets are in the name of your trust.

Action Steps

- Your objective is to set up an estate plan that transfers your assets at your death.

- Your action plan is to consider the options presented in this Chapter so you are prepared to meet with an estate planning attorney.

- Your attorney will prepare the necessary documents that will transfer your assets at your death.

- How to find an attorney, what questions to ask and what information to take to the first meeting are discussed in Chapter Five.

FOUR

TAXES AND "DEATH TAXES"

You will discuss this issue in detail with your attorney. This Chapter will help you prepare for that discussion.

Locate Tax Returns from Prior Years

If, because of disability, you are unable to file your tax returns, your partner or family member will have to file them for you. Your tax returns from prior years will help them.

Locate your tax returns from the past three years. Insert each year's returns in a separate folder and label the folders. File the folders with your other important documents.

Implement a System to Collect Information for Future Returns

Whether you or someone else will be filing next year's tax returns, streamline the process by having information about the year's income and deductions accessible and organized. As you receive 1099s from your employer(s) and financial institutions, insert them in a labeled folder. Also collect information about the assets you sold during the year. At year-end you should have all the information you will need to file your tax returns in the folder. As soon as you have all of the necessary information, schedule a meeting with your tax advisor (or prepare and file the returns yourself.)

Federal Estate Taxes (Death Taxes)

The 2013 tax law authorized an estate tax exemption of $5.25 million with adjustments for inflation in subsequent years. This means that an estate with assets of less than $5.25 million will not be subject to estate taxes (also called the death taxes.)

State Estate Taxes

There are 14 states* and Washington, DC with estate tax exemptions which are **lower** than the federal estate tax exemption. If you live in one of these states, estate taxes could be a concern even if your assets are below the amount of the federal exemption ($5.25 million in 2013.) Tax payers who live in states where their assets may exceed the state estate tax exemption should consult their tax advisor for ways to minimize the tax.

*CT, HI, IL, ME, MD, MA, MN, NJ, NY, OR, RI, TN, VT, WA.

Action Plan

- Set up a system to collect this year's tax information.
- Collect your tax returns from previous years and file them with your important documents.

FIVE

WHO SHOULD PREPARE YOUR ESTATE PLAN?

Who Should Prepare Your Estate Plan?

I recommend that you hire an *experienced* estate planning or elder law attorney to prepare the legal documents that will make up your estate plan. It's penny-wise and pound-foolish to "do-it-yourself."

However, I also recommend that YOU control your estate plan. You tell your attorney what you want your plan to accomplish. Ask your attorney what options you have, including the cost, and the positives and negatives of each option. Then you decide (not your attorney) which options best meet your objectives.

How to Locate an Attorney

You want an estate planning or elder law attorney - an attorney who does estate planning for a living and not as a sideline. Your best source of information is a satisfied customer, so ask family and friends for suggestions. Your accountant and financial planner are also good sources of recommendations.

Another source is your local Bar Association; call and ask for the names of estate planning and elder law attorneys in your area.

Cost of the Initial Consultation

Most estate planning and elder law attorneys do not charge for an initial consultation. Take advantage of a no cost consultation. It will give you the opportunity to judge whether you feel comfortable with the attorney and what his or her fees will be for the documents that you need prepared.

I'm sorry to say that some attorneys do not treat their clients well. If you are not treated respectfully by the attorney and staff; if you are kept waiting for an unreasonable amount of time; if fees are not readily and thoroughly explained; if your estate plan cannot be done in a timely manner or if your phone calls are not returned promptly, find another attorney. There are lots of us out there.

Questions to Ask the Attorney

1. Is estate planning your primary area of practice?

2. How do you charge, flat fee or hourly?

3. If the charge is hourly, what is your best estimate of the total fee?

4. If I have questions will I be able to contact you personally by phone or email?

5. Do you return calls or emails promptly?

6. If you will be drafting a revocable living trust, will you also prepare the documents that will transfer my assets to the trust? Is that included in the fee for the trust or is there an additional cost? **If the attorney will not prepare the documents that transfer your assets to your trust, find another attorney!**

7. How long will the process take from start to finish? If you are about to take a trip and want your estate plan in place before you leave, be sure you tell the attorney at your first meeting.

Before You Meet with an Attorney

Go to www.wsbforms.com/single/and download and fill in the forms in the "Take to the Meeting with an Estate Planning Attorney" section. Fill in the blanks and take them to your first meeting with an estate planning attorney.

Action Steps

- Ask family, friends or co-workers for the name of an estate planning or elder law attorney.
- Schedule an appointment with the attorney and confirm that the initial consultation is free.
- Before you meet with the attorney go to www.wsbforms.com/single/ and download the forms in the "Take to the Meeting with an Estate Planning Attorney" section. Fill in the blanks and take the forms to the meeting with the attorney.
- Meet with the attorney and discuss your objectives and your options.
- If you like the attorney, feel satisfied that you understand your options and the fee is fair, engage the attorney to prepare the documents needed to create your estate plan.
- Put the documents in a safe place. Tell your partner or family member where to find the documents and make certain they can access them.

ONLY ONE OF THE NEXT THREE CHAPTERS APPLIES TO YOU. GO DIRECTLY TO THE CHAPTER THAT DISCUSSES YOUR SITUATION.

SIX

ESTATE PLANNING IF YOU OR YOUR PARTNER HAVE MINOR CHILDREN

You will discuss your family structure in detail with your attorney. This Chapter will help you prepare for that discussion.

What is an Estate Plan for a Couple with Minor Children?

Your attorney will prepare documents that accomplish the following:

1. Name a guardian or guardians for minor children;
2. Name a trusted person to manage the children's money;
3. Implement a Trust or Will that protects the children's inheritance;
4. Name a trusted person to make medical decisions for you if you are unable to make decisions for yourself;
5. Name a trusted person to manage your finances if you become disabled.

What's the Difference Between a Guardian and a Trustee?

A guardian is responsible for the child. A trustee is responsible for the child's money.

How You Name a Guardian

You name a guardian or guardians for children in a Will.

Who to Choose as Guardian

The following information will help you select a guardian for minor children. It's sensible to talk to the person(s) you have in mind to make certain they are willing to act as your children's guardian before your attorney prepares the documents.

Most parents strive to name a guardian who shares their values. Elements to consider include the proposed guardian's religious background, lifestyle and living situation.

Since the financial responsibility will rest with a trustee, the guardian's financial qualifications are of lesser importance. Nevertheless your child will certainly be influenced by the guardian's behavior so choosing a person who is financially responsible is important. However if the person named as guardian is also qualified to manage the child's or children's money, the guardian can also be the trustee.

Although nothing prohibits you from appointing someone who resides in another state, take residency into consideration especially if the proposed guardian lives far away from other family members.

Individual vs. a Couple

Parents often name a married couple to be guardians. Consider, however, who would remain the guardian in the event the couple divorces or one member of the couple dies. Often when pressed on this issue, "my sister and brother-in-law" is really "my sister." In the event of your sister's death, do you want your brother-in-law or someone else to be the guardian? Your Will should reflect your true preference by naming only the desired individual or individuals. Nevertheless if a couple is appropriate name them.

A Sibling

You can name an adult child to act as the guardian for your younger children. Although this may help maintain family continuity, it's a substantial responsibility for the older child. In addition to the enormous change moving from the role of older sibling to the role of stand-in parent, the responsibility associated with acting as guardian may put too much pressure on the siblings' relationship. In seeking the best solution for the younger children, this plan has the potential to cause unintended harm to the older child.

How to Protect Your Children's Inheritance

1. Living Trust

As previously discussed, a Living Trust names who is to receive your assets after your death and who is to administer the trust (the trustee).

As the trustee and beneficiary, you manage and have full use of the trust assets during your lifetime. If you become incompetent and at your death, the person you've named as your successor trustee takes over.

Your attorney will transfer your assets to your trust by changing the title of the asset from your name into the name of your trust.

At your death, your successor trustee will use the trust assets for your children (and your partner if you so choose) following the guidelines that you have specified in the trust. For example, you may direct your trustee to use the trust assets for your children's support, health, education and welfare. Your guidelines may be quite general or very specific.

The trust will also tell the trustee when to distribute the trust assets that have not been used for the child's health, education etc. You can direct the trustee to make a lump sum payment at the age you specify.

Or you can direct the trustee to make two or more installment payments. Most parents choose to keep the children's inheritance in trust until their children are 21-30 years or older.

Children with Special Needs

If you have a child with "special needs" who receives or may receive government benefits, an inheritance may make the child ineligible for those benefits. A Living Trust with *specific special needs provisions* will safeguard the child's benefits.

Selecting a Trustee

The trustee will be the person responsible for managing and distributing your child's inheritance. Therefore, he or she should have successful financial and investment experience <u>and</u> share your views about money.

The guardian and trustee may be the same person but they don't have to be. The decision is yours. If the guardian and trustee are not the same person, keep in mind that they will have to peacefully co-exist for the benefit of your children for what could be a long time.

Age is also a factor. While the children's grandparents may be the best choice today, as they get older, they may no longer be the best choice.

If your trust will continue after your children turn 18, the guardian will be out of the picture but the Trustee will continue until your youngest child reaches the age you specified in the Trust.

Always, Always Name Backup Guardians and Trustees

For all the reasons I've discussed above, I emphasize naming backups for both the guardian and trustee. Better still, review and revise (if necessary) your estate plan regularly. If you've named grandparents as guardian and/or trustee and that's no longer in your children's best interests, revise your estate plan documents.

Revisions are usually not expensive because you are amending your current documents rather than starting from scratch.

Other Reasons for Using a Living Trust

Trusts are used for reasons other than protecting the finances of minor children. Trusts are used to safeguard governmental benefits that are or may be received by disabled children. You can provide for your partner's health and support in a trust. And trusts, if properly funded, avoid probate.

2. A Will that Creates a Trust at Your Death, Testamentary Trust

A Will that creates a trust at your death (a Testamentary Trust) is an economical alternative to a Living Trust. A Testamentary Trust will accomplish most of the same objectives as a Living Trust. A Living Trust goes into effect while you're alive. A Testamentary Trust goes into effect at your death because it's part of your Will.

Summary of Your Estate Plan

Your estate plan must include a Will because that's how you name guardians for your children. You must then decide to have either a Living Trust or include a Testamentary Trust in the Will. Either option will protect your children's finances. You may, however, have other important objectives that can only be satisfied by a Living Trust. Discuss these options in detail with your attorney.

Final Steps in the Estate Planning Process

Once you have an estate plan in place there are four more steps to take:

1. Place your original will, trust, etc. in a safe place.

2. Inform the person(s) you've named as guardian and trustee, power of attorney, executor or personal representative where they will find

the documents at your death.

3. Make sure that person can access the documents. For example, if you keep these documents in a safe deposit box, will they be able to gain access to the box? If the name of the person who will be managing your affairs is not on the box at your death, they won't have access to your documents.

4. Attach an up-to-date Inventory of your assets and debts to your Will or Trust.

Action Steps

- Ask family, friends or co-workers for the name of an estate planning attorney.
- Schedule an appointment with the attorney and confirm that the initial consultation is free.
- Before you meet with the attorney ask your intended guardian and trustee if they are willing.
- Go to www.wsbforms.com/single/ and download the forms in the "Take to the Meeting with an Estate Planning Attorney" section. Fill in the blanks and take them to your first meeting with an estate planning attorney.
- Meet with the attorney and discuss your objectives and your options to meet those objectives. Take your Inventory of assets and debts to the meeting.
- If you like the attorney, feel satisfied that you understand your options and the fee is fair, engage the attorney to prepare the documents needed to meet your objectives and create your estate plan.
- Put the documents in a safe place. Tell your partner where to find the documents and make certain they can access them.

A Parental Consent Form for Minor Children and a Medical Information Form for Minor Children are available at www.wsbforms.com/single.

SEVEN

ESTATE PLANNING IF YOU OR YOUR PARTNER HAVE ADULT CHILDREN

You will discuss your family structure in detail with your attorney. This Chapter will help you prepare you for that discussion.

What is an Estate Plan for a Couple with Adult Children?

Your attorney will prepare documents that accomplish the following:

1. Name a trusted person to make medical decisions for you if you are unable to make decisions for yourself;
2. Name a trusted person to manage your finances if you become disabled;
3. Transfer your assets to the intended recipients at your death. You have five options:

- Beneficiary Designation;

- Joint Ownership;

-Will;

-No Will;

-Living Trust.

Depending on your circumstances, needs and desires, there are advantages and disadvantages to each of these options. For example, if you have one or two beneficiaries and the appropriate types of assets, using beneficiary designations and joint ownership may be an economical and effective method of transferring your assets at your death. However, use caution when transferring assets by joint ownership. See Chapter 3.

On the other hand, if a child has predeceased you, you may (or may not) want your deceased child's share to go to his or her children (your grandchildren). In that case a living trust is the most effective method of transferring your assets.

If you have an adult child with special needs, a revocable living trust with very specific provisions will safeguard any governmental benefits your child receives or may receive in the future.

It may be extremely important to you that probate is avoided at your death. If so, you do not want to transfer your assets by Will.

And you may wish to provide for your partner as well as, or instead of, your children. If so, a revocable living trust, which you can amend at any time, may be the most effective method to accomplish your goal.

As you can see, estate planning is **NOT** "one size fits all." That's why I urge you to engage an *experienced* estate planning attorney to prepare your documents.

Final Steps in the Estate Planning Process

Once you have an estate plan in place there are four more steps to take:

1. Place your original will, trust, powers of attorney, etc. in a safe place.

2. Inform the person(s) you've named as trustee, power of attorney, executor or personal representative where they will find the documents at your death or disability.

3. Make sure that person can access the documents. For example, if you keep these documents in a safe deposit box, will they be able to gain access to the box? If the name of the person who will be managing your affairs is not on the box at your death, they won't have access to your documents.

4. Attach an up-to-date Inventory of your assets and debts to your Will or Trust.

Action Steps

- Ask family, friends or co-workers for the name of an estate planning or elder law attorney.
- Schedule an appointment with the attorney and confirm that the initial consultation is free.
- Before you meet with the attorney go to www.wsbforms.com/single/ and download the forms in the "Take to the Meeting with an Estate Planning Attorney" section. Fill in the blanks and take them to your first meeting with the estate planning attorney.
- Meet with the attorney and discuss your objectives and your options.
- If you like the attorney, feel satisfied that you understand your options and the fee is fair, engage the attorney to prepare the documents needed to create your estate plan.
- Put the documents in a safe place. Tell your partner or family where to find the documents and make certain they can access them.

EIGHT

ESTATE PLANNING IF NEITHER PARTNER HAS CHILDREN

You will discuss your family structure in detail with your attorney. This Chapter will help you prepare for that discussion.

Estate Planning When Neither Partner has Children is Critical

Why is it critical? If you die without an estate plan in place, your assets will go to your closest living relative(s).

Who are your closest living relatives, legally defined as your "heirs at law?" Usually (each state has its own laws that answer this question) it's a parent or parents if they survive you. If not, grandparents if they survive you. If not, it's siblings if they survive you. If none of your siblings survive you, it will be the children of deceased siblings, your nieces and nephews.

That means everything you've worked for and saved could go to someone you haven't seen in years and maybe don't even know (or know but don't like.) It's foolish to put this off.

What is an Estate Plan when Neither Partner has Children?

Your attorney will prepare the documents that accomplish the following:

1. Name a trusted person to make medical decisions for you if you are unable to make decisions for yourself;
2. Name a trusted person to manage your finances if you become disabled;
3. Transfer your assets to the individuals of your choice at your death. You have four options:

- Beneficiary Designation;

- Joint Ownership;

-Will;

-Living Trust.

Final Steps in the Estate Planning Process

Once you have an estate plan in place there are four more steps to take:

1. Place your original will, trust, powers of attorney, etc. in a safe place.

2. Inform the person(s) you've named as trustee, power of attorney, executor or personal representative where they will find the documents at your death or disability.

3. Make sure that person can access the documents. For example, if you keep these documents in a safe deposit box, will they be able to gain access to the box? If the name of the person who will be managing your affairs is not on the box at your death, they won't have access to your documents.

4. Attach an up-to-date Inventory of your assets and debts to your Will or Trust.

Action Steps

- Ask family, friends or co-workers for the name of an estate planning or elder law attorney.
- Schedule an appointment with the attorney and confirm that the initial consultation is free.
- Before you meet with the attorney go to www.wsbforms.com/single/ and download the forms in the "Take to the Meeting with an Estate Planning Attorney" section. Fill in the blanks and take them to your first meeting with the estate planning attorney.
- Meet with the attorney and discuss your objectives and your options.
- If you like the attorney, feel satisfied that you understand your options and the fee is fair, engage the attorney to prepare the documents needed to create your estate plan.
- Put the documents in a safe place. Tell your partner or family where to find the documents and make certain they can access them.

NINE

NOW THAT YOU HAVE YOUR AFFAIRS IN ORDER, KEEP THEM IN ORDER

Keep Your Affairs Up-To-Date

Now that your financial and legal affairs are in order, keep them up-to-date.

Schedule periodic reviews of:

Assets and debts,

Insurance policies,

Pension\retirement plans,

Estate plan,

Tax matters.

Review these issues yearly and at all family events that change your circumstances, i.e births, death, employment changes, retirement and the purchase or sale of significant assets.

Schedule Reviews

Incorporate periodic reviews of your financial and legal affairs into your day planner or diary system. But reminding yourself to review a specific financial or legal matter is useless if you don't actually review it and make any necessary changes.

The Location of Your Documents and Other Information

Your objectives are to:

1. Provide information about your doctors, other health personnel and your medications.

2. Provide information about the people to contact in an emergency.

3. Provide information about your financial and legal advisors.

4. Provide information about a prearranged funeral and\or burial.

Go to www.wsbforms.com/single/ and download the Location of Important Documents form. Fill in the information and then place the list in a secure but accessible place. Tell your partner or family where to find the information and make certain they can gain access. For example, if you place the list in your safe deposit box, be sure your partner or family member know where the box is, where to find the key and are named on the bank's signature card.

Records Stored in Your Computer

If some of your records are stored in your computer:

Make a backup of these records and put the backup in a safe place; *a place that you will remember.*

Prepare a set of instructions for your partner or family so they will be able to access this information. A detailed computer file of important information is useless if your partner doesn't know it exists or knows it exists but can't find it or gain access to it. **Pay special attention to passwords if you bank on-line.**

Action Plan

- Schedule and actually review: Assets and Debts, Estate Tax liability, Insurance, Retirement and Estate Plan.
- Make changes as necessary.
- Attach an up-to-date Inventory of your assets and debts, life insurance policies and retirement plans to your estate plan documents.
- Inform your partner or family of the location of the safe place and make certain they can access the documents.
- Inform your partner or family about documents stored on your computer and how to access the documents.

Get Started!

"Knowledge is Power" but only if the knowledge prompts action. That's why this estate planning guide provides not only accurate up-to-date information but also the action steps required to achieve your objectives.

As in most important undertakings the first step is always the most difficult. But once you get started everything will quickly fall into place. Your reward will be the peace of mind that comes from knowing that you have made things as easy as possible for your partner and that your affairs are in order.

ABOUT THE AUTHOR

Julie Calligaro has been an estate planning and probate attorney for 30 years. An estate planning attorney is really in the peace of mind business because once you have your affairs in order, you will experience peace of mind.

Ms. Calligaro was named an Estate and Gift Taxation Lawyer of the year by "*dbusiness,*" Detroit's premier business journal, in 2010. And has been a member of the Ethics Committee at Henry Ford Wyandotte Hospital for 17 years.